Invocations

PRAYERS AND BLESSINGS
TO ILLUMINATE YOUR LIFE

HAYLEY HUNTER HINES

First paperback edition February 2022

Book Interior and E-book Design by Amit Dey | amitdey2528@gmail.com

ISBN 979-8-9857534-1-7 (paperback)
ISBN 979-8-9857534-0-0 (ebook)

www.soulsparkleliving.com

Table of Contents

Introduction

From The Author

"Grace comes into the soul as the morning into the world; first dawning, then a light, and at last, the sun in its full, excellent brightness."

— Thomas Adams

Sweet ones, the greatest gift we can give to the world is the light from our own souls. Now more than ever, we must embody the greatest levels of light and unconditional love. There is an exciting transformation of human consciousness happening right now, and we have an extraordinary opportunity to maximize our purpose in a whole new way.

It is time to step into the truth of who you are.

Remember that you are loved. You are light. You were born to be a blessing to the world.

You are here to light the way for others, to show them who they truly are as well.

I'm inviting you to join me on the journey, and I'm calling you forth into the next iteration and evolution of you.

Are you ready to transform and step up in new and exciting ways? To find the strength to make the decisions that will support your well-being and right to thrive? There is nothing you have ever done that could make you unworthy of divine intervention, grace, and love.

My hope is that, within these pages, you will feel seen, known, loved, and most of all, connected... connected to the truth of who you are, to the light that you are in the world, and to each and every heart and soul that is on this journey of discovery with you. I hope this book will support you on your journey to become "like a city on the hill" - a beacon of love and grace. I hope you find this to be a rich and inspirational guide to living a happy and meaningful life filled with abundance and healthy relationships.

My love for bringing more light into the world, my fascination with esoteric and mystical ideas, and my obsession with the point where science and spiritual technologies and teachings meet. This book was written because of all of these things.

I am a teacher of the *Way of Love,* and I do this by combining the mystical teachings of Jesus, the Seven Sacred

Seals and Sacred Flames, Sacred Soul Alignments, and the spiritual technology of Kundalini Yoga.

This book is a culmination of the above practices, focusing on the Seven Sacred Flames combined with invocations, prayers, and blessings to feel enriched, enlivened, and fueled with courage to move beyond your current circumstances and embrace the destiny that is waiting for you.

The Seven Sacred Flames are powerful tools that help us have a deeper understanding of cosmic laws. Our self-realization and God-mastery come from the consistent and persistent application, and they all work together so beautifully. These spiritual technologies and esoteric teachings are used to support you in stepping into your Sovereign Divinity - that sacred space where you stand firmly between your divinity and your humanity.

I created this book to introduce you to these powerful sacred flames along with beautiful invocations, prayers, and blessings and to support you on your spiritual journey. My hope is that as you work with these expressions of love and devotion, you will find truth and peace in your heart and spirit. True spirituality is a state of being, not doing. A pure consciousness that brings you back to love, light, true life, and your divinity.

The Universe wants something extraordinary to happen for you, something beautiful, and something perfect for your own unique destiny in this lifetime. Your heart will burn for it to become real. You will want it with all of your being. Join me on this journey of self-illumination to ignite the light within you so that you can become a beacon for those you are here to love and serve.

Within these pages, you may discover truths so powerful that they will bring tears to your eyes as you explore the deepest desires of your heart. Go ahead and discover them. Delight in them. Let the tears fall if they need to. Give yourself permission to experience them because that is where the magic lives. Soften into receiving the blessing that is available for you here.

Take some time each day to invoke these flames speak these prayers and blessings. Breathe them in and wrap yourself in these loving energies. Ask for guidance and clarity for the path ahead. This is the work we must do to prepare our bodies, minds, and spirits for the ascension on earth at this time. It will take all of us to participate in creating the new world. We must think, speak and act in a way that allows our vibration to align with that of the ascension timeline.

Before we can be completely whole and express the fullness of the light of the I AM presence within our sacred heart, and we must heal all aspects of ourselves on deeper levels. True healing is available using one of the Seven Sacred Flames each day until we are able to reflect our divine perfection. We want to stay focused on raising our frequency and vibration to the highest levels of love, grace, and forgiveness which we can do in many ways, but meditation and contemplation are both powerful paths to access this next level of consciousness, which creates our reality.

These sacred energies work together with each other and it is of benefit to include all of them in some way throughout your week. One way to work intimately with the seven rays is to focus on the amplified ray each day.

While you are certainly not limited to this, you may find that it may bring greater ease and grace to your life and will balance and amplify the energies in each of the associated chakra. In Sanskrit, a chakra means an energy center, and ideally, all of our chakras are open and clear for optimum energy, function, and vitality. Working with each of the rays will help you stay clear, balanced, and capable of experiencing an amazing level of radiance.

Remember that you are a channel of grace and here to serve humanity by loving yourself unconditionally and helping others to do the same. You are the living embodiment of unconditional love and grace.

May you be open to the impossible made possible.

May you fall in love with yourself and your life in ways you didn't realize were possible.

May you step into your Sovereign Divinity and be filled with the light of Divine love.

If you are seeking a personal and collective shift in these exciting and evolutionary times, welcome. It is your destiny to hand out pieces of light so that others may find their way home. We've been waiting for you, love.

> *Blessed be those of you whose heart has chosen to be here now, and blessed is the light that shines now through the beauty of your soul to help others find their way. We are at a choice point, loves. Do you want to step into a whole new reality and dimension, a heaven on earth experience? We are here for such a time as this.*

Definition of terms used in this book

Throughout this book, you will see the terms Invocation, Prayer, Blessing, and God. Below are brief explanations for each:

Invocations are defined as "the action of invoking someone or something" and "a supplication or prayer it implies to call upon God, a god, goddess, or person, etc." When a person calls upon God to ask for something (protection, a favor, his/her spiritual presence in a ceremony, etc.) or simply for worship, this can be done in a pre-established form or with the invoker's own words or actions. It is the act of appealing to a higher authority for help. In its simplest form, the invocation is a prayer or request for the spiritual presence of God in a moment, a ceremony, or an event.

Prayer in the Hebrew Bible is described as "an evolving means of interacting with God, most frequently through a spontaneous, individual, unorganized form of petitioning and/or thanking. Vocal prayer may be spoken or sung. Mental prayer can be either meditation or contemplation.

The basic forms of prayer are praise, a petition (supplication), intercession, and thanksgiving." Marianne Williamson says, "I think of prayer as a spiritual lifeline back to where I most want to be," and that "Prayer is a powerful force that can lift spirits, guide journeys, and heal the heart."

A *blessing* can be described as "a declaration of divine favor, or an invocation imploring divine favor on someone or something; a benediction; a wish of happiness pronounced. ... A means of happiness; that which promotes prosperity and welfare; a beneficent gift."

I hope you will substitute the word for God that feels best for you throughout this book. If you feel more comfortable and connected to the word Universe, Source, Creator, etc., that is perfect. This book is meant to be available for all that feel called to have a deeper connection to the Divinity within.

Chapter 1

Preparing Your Physical Body

*"Health is a state of complete harmony of the
body, mind, and spirit. When one is free from
physical disabilities and mental distractions, the
gates of the soul open."*

BKS Iyengar

Your body is the vessel that allows the opportunity to connect, create magic, and make an impact in the world. Now, more than ever, we must focus our intention on creating the healthiest version of our physical body so we can increase our vibration and the amount of light we can hold.

We live in the space between the darkness and the light and embody the divine living in light and flesh. In order to access the holy higher realms with more ease and grace, we must refine the frequency of our physical body, refine our thoughts and create a more simple way of living

For me personally, this looked like moving toward a primarily plant-based eating style, removing sugar and dairy from my diet, and adding much more movement to my daily routine. If you think about density, meat and animal products are much heavier energetically than plants, so finding the right balance for your body is important to support you on your spiritual path.

Our highest frequency and brightest light will shine when we release and let go of all the things holding us back, weighing us down, and keeping us small. This could be unhealthy foods or habits. It could be toxic relationships or interactions, limiting thoughts, beliefs, and possibly outdated oaths, vows, and contracts.

The light determines the aging of our physical body we can hold. If we want to grow more beautiful as we grow older, we must learn (and work at), raising our vibration to a high level of love and harmony and maintaining this frequency throughout our lives.

How do we do this? We focus on it.

When we put our full attention on something and pour our love into it, we immediately begin to create and bring it into our world.

To begin, I encourage you to shift your focus to your I AM presence and allow yourself to naturally receive the light as it fills you. You can begin by visualizing a beautiful golden light pouring through your entire body and all body systems. I recommend doing this practice for five minutes, 2-3 times a day which will actively accelerate the frequency and vibration of your body.

Think about ways you can incorporate more movement in your everyday life. Can you create a standing work-station instead of sitting all day? Can you go for a quick walk in the morning or when you get home from work? Maybe a few laps around the office with your co-workers? If you enjoy yoga, perhaps you can do a personal practice at home and then find a studio you enjoy for an extended class on the weekend.

Review the products you are using/consuming regularly. Are you drinking filtered water? What foods are you nour-ishing your body with? If you desire a deeper level of radi-ance and vitality, begin to visualize that you already have it. Imagine your mind being calm and clear; your body strong and healthy; every cell is filled with light; feeling and knowing the energies of God are flowing through you and creating a gorgeous glow about you.

Declaration

I am gently, powerfully restored to my inherent divine radiance-ready to live my life with love and filled with trust, patience, boldness, and sweet affection.

PRAYER

For restoration and vibrance:

May I be restored to my inherent divine radiance, ready to live my life with a heart full of love, trust, patience, and grace.
I invite in vibrance.
I invite health at a whole new level.
I invite in anything that is in the highest and best for me at this time.

For healing:

Loving God, I pray that you will comfort me in my suffering, lend skill to the hands of my healers, and bless the means used for my cure.
Give me such confidence in the power of your grace and healing that I may put my whole trust in you even when I am afraid.

INVOCATION

I now step fully into the healthiest version of myself. My body is balanced, whole, and healthy. I am radiant, strong, and powerful.

Chapter 2

Create Your Spiritual Practice

*"I feel that the essence of spiritual practice is
your attitude toward others. When you have
a pure, sincere motivation, then you have the
right attitude toward others based on kindness,
compassion, love, and respect."*

Dalai Lama

*B*eginning each day with an intentional moment of stillness, contemplation, and connection to God prepares our minds and hearts to stay open, loving, and ready for whatever comes our way. Creating a daily spiritual practice is the cornerstone that everything else in your life builds upon.

The deep connection to Source within you is the key and pathway to freedom and peace. When you learn how to tap into and connect with your inner wisdom and guidance, you will discover a whole new way of showing up in your relationships, conversations, communities, and world. This practice of accessing your inner connection to the divine is the most beautiful gift you can give yourself.

This journey is designed to ignite the light within you so that you become a beacon of love and hope for those you are meant to serve in this lifetime. This includes your family, your community, friends, and loved ones. With the consistent practice of these teachings, you will fall in love with yourself and your life in a way you never realized was available for you.

If you are just beginning your journey on the spiritual path, welcome. If you have had a spiritual practice for years, I welcome you here too. We are each on a different journey but are equal and beautiful in our own way. I am so happy you have found your way here and am excited for you to be on the journey with us.

You can begin by creating your personal morning ritual/ routine. It may help to gather a few sacred items as you start out. You may want a new journal, your favorite pen, a beautiful candle, a few of your favorite crystals and a cozy blanket. You may also want to keep close other items such as oracle cards, a special spiritual book, or anything else that helps you feel connected to Creator/God/Source energy. Create a space in your home where you can be quiet and undisturbed.

You may start by lighting your candle, signaling that this time is holy and sacred, then close your eyes and take a deep breath in and a long, slow exhale.

One way to start is, to begin with meditation, quieting your mind into stillness. From this place of stillness, we are able to find clarity on things we may be struggling with, and ultimately, a place of calm and peace. From this place, we are able to access a connection with our Divine self, our holy inner being, and tap into the mind and heart of God. When we approach our practice from this place, our inner knowing can be activated, allowing us to think, feel, and imagine from a higher place, your higher self. You can simply call forth your "I AM" presence and allow yourself to step into your Christ consciousness, trusting that your request will be met.

A lovely practice called automatic writing can be an incredible blessing and source of clarity. This practice is as simple as asking a question and then allowing yourself to write whatever comes to you without limiting yourself or editing what you have written. This is a beautiful practice to include each day and allows us to stay in alignment with what God has planned for us.

You can start by asking a few simple questions and journaling the responses. Maybe the question is, "What do I need to know today? How can I serve today? Who do I need to connect with today?" Write whatever comes to mind.

When you feel complete and ready to move on with your day, put your right hand on your heart and your left hand on your belly. Take a deep breath, and a long, slow exhale and repeat three times. When you feel ready, you can open your eyes.

Chapter 3

The Illumination Flame of Wisdom: Sunday

*"I will love the light for it shows me the way,
yet I will endure the darkness for it shows
me the stars."*

Og Mandino

*N*ow we begin the journey of the Sacred Flames with the Illumination Ray. We begin here because the power of this ray is amplified on Sunday, and the focus of this ray is connecting with the Mind of God.

When we invoke the Yellow Ray of Illumination, we increase our light expand our potential for reconnecting to the Mind of God and our divinity. The Illumination Ray is a brilliant golden yellow, and the initiation of this ray allows us to become aware of all the limiting beliefs we have carried about who we really are. This ray corresponds with the Crown chakra, and when you begin working with this ray, the crown chakra begins to be illuminated and expands your ability to reconnect with the true Mind of God.

Within each of us, we carry our human brain *and* the Mind of God. Our human brains are controlled by our ego and can be a source of fear, negative thoughts, and separation consciousness.

We are able to transform this, though, and unite our human mind with the Mind of God, which represents Universal consciousness and has limitless potential. We can release our old thoughts and beliefs that no longer serve us with true wisdom and surrender.

As we walk the path toward our ascension, we will eventually merge completely and experience all aspects of our divinity. By invoking this Ray of Illumination, we can help our minds transform and nourish our hearts and souls with beauty, see God in everything, and create love and connection, allowing our transformed mind to align with our Sacred Heart.

We must access the intelligence and power of our hearts in ways that many have never been able to do before. The ongoing work with the prayers and invocations here, along with any others you may use, will allow you to access the beauty and the blessing of your heart and to keep it open even when it is challenging or even painful to do so. Our human minds were created to serve our hearts, as it is our hearts that are connected to the Divine Mind of God. We must embrace unconditional love and grace for ourselves to radiate that into the world. When enough people act from God's mind through their hearts, we will create a ripple of change and the world we want to live in.

ACTIVATION

(Repeat 3, 6, or 9 times)

> I call forth my beloved I AM Presence and the Light of my Soul.

> I pour out my love and devotion to you, asking to be restored to my eternal Divine Blueprint. As I AM renewed in your Embrace, I feel the Peace from the light of your unending Love.

> *"A man must have a spiritual vision in order to perceive and comprehend the spiritual light of illumination. Then a magnificent world will be opened to him, a world in which illumination reigns. This illumination is both intelligent and alive, and all the great mystics who kindle it within themselves are able to see a boundless world, pulsating with the softest, most delicate and beautiful colors which fill their souls with streams of life."*

> **Beans Duono**

PRAYER

Allow me to remember the deepest truth of who I am, of the love and light within my heart and soul, my divinity within me.

Please bring me peace and grace so that I may extend that grace to all of those I meet today in whatever way they show up.

May I be a blessing to someone in need of my love, forgiveness, and compassion.

And may I bring all of my radiant light into the world with these words and this prayer.

And so it is.

INVOCATION

I invoke the illumination ray and call forth the mind of God. I aspire to embody the full expression of God and devote all of myself to the service of that end.

I bring tranquility, love, harmony, and peace to all life in all ways.

I will walk gently upon earth and through the Universe, knowing that my body is a sacred temple where the Holy Spirit dwells, bringing peace and illumination to life everywhere.

Chapter 4

The Blue Ray of the
Will of God: Monday

*T*here is nothing more important in our lives in this present moment than our personal healing and spiritual development. We often get distracted by so many other things in our lives, but our primary path for ascension is following the Will of God with our ability to surrender.

How will we know we are on the "right path" of the highest timeline available for us unless we allow ourselves to be guided and redirected as needed, staying unattached to the outcome? The shortest path to the home of the divinity within us is to surrender to God's Will.

Your soul has a deep desire to have you experience all that you were meant to before you came earthside. The experience was designed to be one of absolute peace, love, joy, abundance, and ease by birthright as a divine being. Instead, there is sadness, suffering, pain, and fear until we realize another way.

"The Will of God is not outside of you. It is simply the God you are and that you have always been, although you tend to temporarily forget when you are in physical incarnation. Your divine Presence is totally omniscient, omnipresent, and omnipotent and can fulfill your desires instantly. You have forgotten that you are nothing less than an expression of this great I AM, incarnated in a human experience. You came here to attain soul perfection and expand your own divinity to the fullness of your God-Mastery and Wisdom. You are here seeking advanced enlightenment and total spiritual freedom. You are here to become an unlimited God in all planes of existence." p.17 Seven Sacred Flames.

We must be willing to embrace all the parts of ourselves that we have not loved or honored over all of our souls' incarnations and fully trust and surrender to the path toward our divine perfection. We can choose a new way of living that releases our resistance to the truth of who we are. We must trust that what is happening on the planet is a catalyst for humanity to reach the level of awakening required at this time. We must trust the beauty of the light at the end of this tunnel we find ourselves in.

This ray is connected to the throat chakra and is a radiant royal blue. This is the ray of divine power and leadership and is frequently misused. We are to use the power of this ray to speak words of compassion and love, to encourage one another and lift each other. Our words can be such a blessing when used in this way.

The best possible way for you to serve humanity at this time is to release all fear and judgement and fully surrender with love to what is unfolding, and encourage others to do the same.

You are here for your soul's growth and must do the work required to evolve your consciousness to attain mastery. Let your heart listen to the call of your soul, and you will know your true purpose here on earth at this time.

Chapter 5

The Rose Pink Ray of Divine Love: Tuesday

"To be born in love is to serve all beings and all creation. Real lovers serve ardently, hopefully, and in an ecstasy of awe. Look for the happiness of the servant of love. All the joys of the world are nothing to it."

~ Rumi

This rose pink ray is the flame that represents Cosmic and Unconditional love. Working with this flame can amplify the beauty of your soul through compassion, selflessness, surrender, intuitive development, and creativity. This brilliant pink ray of love opens our hearts through creative modalities like art and music. This flame can help you create all the desires of your heart!

Our human minds were designed to always be at the service of the heart. Our hearts are connected to the Mind of

God, and until we reach a state of union within ourselves, our ego-mind needs to be consciously at the service of the heart.

We can become spiritually ignorant when we spend all of our time and energy in our human mind vs. our heart. You may know incredibly intelligent people but have no spiritual wisdom, and they use their intelligence in service to their ego instead of seeking their Oneness with all that is.

When we change our perspective to embrace and embody the energies of love, peace, and harmony for ourselves first, then we radiate to others around us by simply being who we are. Doing this inner work is the greatest contribution you can make for your family, community, and world. When entire populations start accessing the Mind of God through the Heart, our policies and politics will begin to change and mirror this new consciousness of the collective. As we collectively evolve, we will have the wisdom to elect different leaders who reflect this new consciousness level.

In order to fully understand the true meaning of love, we can work with the third ray, which is the three-fold flame of love that lives within our hearts and signifies that we are divine beings and that God has a plan to use that to bless others. The flame of love is one of the Seven Flames of God acting on the planet for humanity. Love is the glue and the vibration that keeps all of God's creations functioning together in perfect order, harmony, and majestic beauty. Love is the ultimate healer and regenerator. The love we are working with here is pure divine love and is the one virtue of the Universal I AM presence with which all others blend. As time goes on, love will be the highest expression of God's nature, and it will also be the highest expression of man.

As we climb the ladder of spiritual evolution, there is a constant expansion of light, virtues, and gifts of God through every Divine Being who has been created. When you allow the consciousness of divine love to rule your life, you become a magnet for love and, most importantly, to radiate this love to all of life around you.

One way to expand this love within you is to *practice gratitude*. When you express your gratitude to God and your Higher Self, you will expand your blessings. The laws of creation, manifestation, and multiplication are fueled and activated by the feeling and expression of gratitude. If you can stay in this flame of love and be grateful, you will avoid those who cannot.

We can never underestimate the power of our heart flame. When we allow it to be ignited by the fires of our love, it becomes the power that moves mountains and the blessings that pour from our hearts through the glorious voice of our Presence. The light shines so brightly it illuminates the pathway for others to find love. It is the energy that fuels our power center to create miracles of healing and every perfect gift available to us.

We must become passionate about becoming love incarnate by increasing that fire within our sacred hearts. This love has to become our primary goal, constant motivation, and the main reason for being.

This flame is connected to our heart chakra, magnifying the Love of the divine and human self. Love's divine qualities are, among others, compassion, mercy, charity, and the desire to be God in action through the love of the Holy Spirit. Love is a power, a vibration, an essence. It is the most priceless element, and it transcends time and space.

Our love is our greatest strength and the most important God-attribute that we can cultivate and develop. When we develop this God-given power, He will have the power to create and bring forth whatever his purified spiritual vision of love beholds. Remember that all relationships serve a single purpose: the possibility of expanding our capacity to love.

Remember that we are anchors of the light and portals to awakening consciousness. When we choose to be here, it is safe to shine. The vibration of heavenly perfection can enter for the well-being of all. The awakening consciousness will come in a fury of grace. Our job is to be the bringers of light. Stay loving. Stay open. Trust that things always work out for you. Always, in all ways.

Every relationship is an opportunity to fulfill your higher purpose in your life

Chapter 6

The Green Ray of Healing and Manifestation: Wednesday

"Gratitude is one of the strongest and most transformative states of being. It shifts your perspective from lack to abundance and allows you to focus on the good in your life, which in turn pulls more goodness into your reality."

Jen Sincero

*I*f you are in need of healing, you can invoke the green ray or ask to visit the Great Jade Temple in the etheric realm where this immortal flame resides. This is an incredible opportunity to amplify your etheric body, allowing you to experience a much higher vibration and level of light within your physical body.

This ray can also support healing in the emotional and mental body so you can back into complete balance. We are meant to live in peace and joy, but we often carry emotional trauma, fears, and beliefs that keep us from the most blissful states of being and create physical manifestations of these emotional wounds. Work with this ray and you can clear and release the energies inside of you that don't allow you to see and feel your true, divine self.

As we walk this path of ascension, we are called to completely transform to pure love and pure light. When we set the intention and are consistent with our inner work and call upon our higher self, guides, and all beings of the light, we can make our way back to wholeness in body, mind, and spirit. When we keep our minds and hearts open, healing will unfold with ease and grace.

Everything you desire is available for you now. You simply need to call it forth. All the love, health, and limitless abundance you wish to receive lies within you. When you activate the divine essence that is alive in you, all you can know and require to manifest your daily lives as divine beings become available.

Stepping into Abundance

A PRAYER FOR FINANCES

My finances are resurrected with ease and grace. I am safe. I am always taken care of, always, in all ways. I am supported and have more than enough. Money flows to me with ease and grace. I am willing to see things differently and open myself to absolute abundance. I am a magnet for million-dollar opportunities. I'm stepping into a new way of being, and I'm available for magic and miracles. I am blessed beyond measure. Clearing the past makes room for new desires to take form. I am worthy of magic and miracles. My work is powerful and worthy of high compensation. Money comes to me with ease and grace. More than enough opulence, abundance, and extraordinary wealth.

A PRAYER FOR MONEY

Creator, I am thankful in advance for receiving xyz amount with absolute ease and grace. I am a magnet for million-dollar opportunities. I now clear all limiting beliefs to make room for new desires to take form. Money is energy and vibration, and it flows to me with ease and grace. I am worthy of the money I desire. I am moving into new levels of abundance. It is safe to receive all my desires. I am available for pure money magic and miracles around every corner.

BLESSING

You have created me in Your image. Let Your gifts abundantly fill my cup until it overflows. Bless me with the riches of righteousness and the prosperity of faith so that my treasure will be stored up in heaven. Amen

INVOCATION 1

I am worthy of magic and miracles. My work is powerful and worthy of high compensation. Money comes to me with ease and grace. More than enough opulence, abundance, and extraordinary wealth.

INVOCATION 2

I am a magnet for million-dollar opportunities. I now clear all limiting beliefs to make room for new desires to take form. Money is energy and vibration, and it flows to me with ease and grace. I am worthy of the money I desire. I am moving into new levels of abundance. It is safe to receive all my desires. I am available for pure money magic and miracles around every corner.

Chapter 7

The Golden Ray of Resurrection: Thursday

The golden ray of resurrection is the hope of redemption for the entire human race. This ray elevates the vibration and activates the light within the human body's cells. Resurrection means bringing back or restoring to a normal condition, to wholeness. The way we invoke this powerful flame in our own lives is to simply say the affirmation, "I AM the Resurrection and the Life." feel the energy of this flame grow within you. This is the path to healing on all levels. The world is in need of so much healing right now we must do the work required for wholeness. The powerful flame is free and so easy to use. It was the flame of Resurrection that Jesus used to resurrect his own body in the tomb after his crucifixion. When we need healing for our physical body, we can invoke this flame and take our body to a higher vibrational frequency and restore ourselves to our original divine perfection. When Jesus said, "These and greater things than these shall you do." (John 14:12), this is one of the things he was referring to. Now that humanity has elevated to a new level of consciousness, we can better understand these higher teachings and how to implement them into our lives.

We can use the resurrection flame in a number of ways. We can resurrect our finances, our health, our relationships, etc.

"From the Lord God of my being, I call forth now to receive a great infusion of Resurrection Flame in every cell, atom, and electron in my physical body, my elemental body, and all my subtle bodies. I wish to heal and resurrect all aspects of my life."

Chapter 8

The White Ray
of Ascension: Friday

*T*his beautiful ray appears as a gorgeous white sparkling light and consumes anything not at the frequency of love. Working with this flame changes us in the most glorious way, and once we begin, we will never be the same. The process is less about "doing" and more about becoming who we were meant to be and embracing the truth of who we are and why we are here.

The process of ascension includes the transition into the 5th dimension from the 3rd dimension of our current reality. In order to access the 5th, we must be able to hold that higher 5D frequency at all times. If we desire to complete the journey of ascension and reach a place of self-mastery, radiant health, and perfect peace, we must focus on the presence of God within our hearts.

We are in the midst of the most transformational rise in consciousness that we have ever experienced as a human family. In order to prepare ourselves for this time of transition, we must complete a series of initiations.

The first one includes developing a connection with the divinity within us or our God Presence and the discipline in our daily lives to nurture that connection. Releasing habits and stimulants that limit our connection will be required during this initiation to move forward.

Next, we go through the initiation of learning, where we deepen our understanding of all Universal Laws. This is when our gifts become more developed, and we are able to step even more fully into our purpose and the passions we have been given.

The third is an initiation into unconditional love and compassion for ourselves and humanity. We must demonstrate an ability to live in peace and harmony with others.

Then we move into the initiation of pure-white Light Radiance. We prepare ourselves for this initiation by purifying our minds and bodies as much as we can in order to see ourselves as we truly are.

Our next initiation is that of Consecration. We are wrapped in a golden robe, and our gifts of healing are activated along with the ability to see perfection in others and speak only words of blessing.

The sixth initiation is the Temple of Service, where we are guided by Jesus and Mary Magdalene into deeper wisdom of how best we can serve humanity from a place of selfless service.

After each of these previous initiations has been completed, we are given the opportunity to complete the process with the seventh. With the help of Saint Germain, we are made pure by using the Violet Flame to get rid of all of our old habits and become the embodiment of God's will.

We have been given a beautiful opportunity to transition with more ease and grace than ever before, and we are so supported and so very loved. Everything is possible for our ascension in this lifetime when we commit to the process and hold the intention.

Chapter 9

The Violet Ray of Transmutation: Saturday

*M*any of us were taught to believe that we are poor sinners and unworthy of love and belonging. If we are made in the image of God, how could that possibly be true? In order to embrace the truth of who we are, we must first release all of those beliefs we were taught that are not true and step into the knowing that we were born perfect, worthy, and more than enough. In order to create heaven on earth and anchor in the Seventh Golden Age, we must begin now, and the Violet Flame can help us on our journey.

This ray is a combination of the Blue and Pink ray, and it represents the energy of freedom and transmutation. It can be used through invocation or meditation, visualizing to receive the benefits of this flame in all areas of your life. One main focus of the Violet flame is purification, and it has the ability to release and transmute karma when used consistently and can create a deep level of joy and freedom.

You can invoke the violet flame anytime you feel it would benefit. When I work with the flames, I follow the same process each time. I start with a prayer and imagine myself surrounded by a ball of golden light. Then I ask Archangel Michael to cover me with his radiant blue light and provide protection. I then begin by calling forth my I AM presence and ask for the Violet Flame to surround me, visualizing a purple and indigo fire lighting up inside my heart and burning through anything that is not in alignment with my highest and best.

Once you have worked with this flame for yourself, you can invoke its power for your loved ones, community, and world.

Chapter 10

The Sacred Convergence

"If you're lucky, you find your way into a spiritual community, and you start to find the great teachers of all the ages who said the same thing. There's only love. You're made of love."

Ann Lamott

*T*here is a sacred convergence happening, love. It's a coming together of souls in alignment with a greater cause; soul families finding connecting to lift each other into greater levels of unconditional love and allow each other to shed fear and open our hearts, filling each other up with love, blessings, and grace; to create sacred containers for support, community and most of all, connection.

When I think about what I want most in my life, I think of loving and supportive relationships. We've gone through so much in recent years that we need to feel even more connected to each other in the community than ever before. Have you found a place where you feel fully seen, known, loved, connected, and supported?

Moving forward, our communities will become even more important as we navigate the times we find ourselves in. With the power of the seven sacred flames, along with the support of a loving community, we can shine brighter than ever before and step into our highest level of service to humanity. Let us share our light with the world.

"I will love the light for it shows me the way, yet I will endure the darkness for it shows me the stars."

Og Mandino

A PRAYER FOR COMPASSION FOR OTHERS IN OUR COMMUNITY

May my love and compassion flow through me and to those around me. Give us the compassion and empathy I need to understand what those in my community are going through. Help me to love them well. Help me not judge or condemn, but rather come alongside them to offer support and be Your hands and feet. Amen.

A PRAYER FOR PEACE IN THE WORLD

Beloved I AM Presence, blaze forth now from the heart of beloved Alpha and Omega, into our hearts and minds, glorious waves of golden Flame of Illumination and Peace.

Flood us with the precious oils of universal knowledge and wisdom.

Come now and direct Thy precious light rays of Divine Illumination and Peace into every aspect of our lives.

Flood the Earth and humanity with the golden Flame of Christ Illumination, Understanding, and Peace from the Heart of God in the Great Central Sun.

> *"It is my deepest belief that only Sacred Activism – the fusion of the deepest mystical knowledge, peace, strength, and stamina with calm, focused, and radical action – can possibly be of use now.*
>
> *A mysticism that is only private and self-absorbed leaves the evils of the world intact and does little to halt the suicidal juggernaut of history; activism that is not purified by a profound spiritual vision and psychological self-awareness and rooted in divine truth, wisdom, and compassion will only perpetuate the problem it is trying to solve, whatever it's righteous intentions.*

> *When, however, the deepest and most grounded mystical vision is married to a practical and pragmatic drive to transform all existing political, economic, and social institutions, a holy force and power of wisdom in action are born, a force and power that can re-fashion all things in and under God, and bring humanity, even at this late desperate hour, into harmony with itself."*

Harvey

There is a beautiful evolution happening in the space of traditional activism. A transformation from the old way into a new wave of being. It's the combination of deep passion for change and justice but comes from a place of grounded and anchored love and compassion. Many in the "spiritual community" tend to lean toward more passive responses, sending "light and love" vs. taking inspired action toward justice.

On the other side, people feel judged by the activists telling them that what they are doing/not doing is wrong. But the truth is, there is another way, a way of being "love in action" and is grounded in God/Source/Universe. This is why we need a new way. We need to become Sacred Activists.

Dr. Andrew Harvey has done incredible work in the area of what he calls Sacred Activism. He describes a concept of a third flame. He describes it in a way that makes so much sense, saying that Mystics have an addiction to inner experience and personal ascension but do not impact others, only themselves.

He says that Activists tend to be self-righteous and have noble motives, but they are sometimes done with more judgment less love. The magic happens when we bring these two together into a new "third wave" of sacred activism.

Harvey defines the concept this way: "A sacred activist is someone who is starting to experience the inner joy and outer effectiveness of this force, who knows that the profound crisis the world is in is challenging everyone to act from our deepest compassion and wisdom, and who is committed to being, in the face of growing chaos, suffering, and violence, what Robert Kennedy called "a tiny ripple of hope" and a "center of energy and daring." Andrew Harvey

We must become these tiny ripples of hope in order to create the greatest change in the world. In essence, developing this third flame of sacred activism requires a deep spiritual practice as the core of your life.

A consistent practice of meditation and mindful movement. Other elements of this lifestyle are to live as simply as possible, simplifying our lives and minimizing everything to create more ease and flow, time and space.

I believe we all have something that we are passionate about that can inspire us to serve and give back, and we are happier when we have found it. How do you find the cause or project that is right for you? He suggests that we ask the question, "What of all the causes in the world break your heart? Discover this, and you will find the deepest compassion in your heart.

Hildegard of Bingen, a great Sacred Activist of her time, wrote, "Humanity, full of creative possibilities, is God's work. Humanity is called upon to assist God. Humanity is called to co-create with God."

These words by the great 12th-century Christian woman saint challenge us all, whatever our religious or spiritual belief, to do three linked things: to uncover our own divine nature through prayer and meditation, to attune our hearts and will to the will of God for the transformation of the earth, and to devote and pour out all our God-given life energies in creativity, service, and justice-making so that divine reality can be increasingly embodied in the world.

The greatest joy and peace live in giving our lives to service. We create a third fire of divine love and wisdom in action. When we illuminate our minds, hearts, and bodies, there is nothing impossible for us. When we come together to create communities to support local issues, we become love in action. We connect to ourselves and each other, pray and create change together. When we show up in the world from a place of sacred service and surrender the truth of our actions, we become a blessing to the world and express the highest form of our divinity.

We must commit to daily communion with the divine source within us and receive the strength, grace, and support to do our greatest work in the world and make the biggest impact.

We must serve from a place of gratitude and devotion. We must prepare and nourish our bodies and our minds to do the work we are called to do. We must keep our hearts lit up with compassion for those we are meant to serve.

We must be aware of what is happening in the world and how we can make an impact. Review where and how you are spending your money and time. Where do you feel called to be of service? How can you ground yourself in the light of divine love and grace, done without self-righteousness? This is the heart of sacred activism. "Profound spiritual knowledge with deep radical action to save the planet plus the passion for God and the passion for justice." Harvey. "When we discover the joy of compassionate service, is married to a practical and pragmatic drive to transform our economic, social, and political institutions, a radical and potentially all-transforming holy force is born. I call this radical holy force sacred activism." (Harvey) Reference: The Hope. A Guide to Sacred Activism by Andrew Harvey.

When I ignite this gift, I activate the forces of synchronicity and grace of my outer life. This can only occur when I embrace my own inner nobility and express it through selfless service and unconditional love. Andrew Harvey is a British author, religious scholar, and teacher of mystic traditions, known primarily for his popular nonfiction books on spiritual or mystical themes.

In closing, I hope these invocations and teachings have been a blessing, and I'm so thankful to have you on this journey with me. Please reach out if you have questions or need support navigating the sacred flames. It has been an honor to spend time with you here.

The Great Invocation

From the point of Light within the Mind of God
Let light stream forth into the minds of men.
Let Light descend on Earth.

From the point of Love within the Heart of God
Let love stream forth into the hearts of men.
May Christ Consciousness return to Earth.

From the center where the Will of God is known
Let purpose guide the little wills of men-
The purpose which the Masters know and serve.

From the centre which we call the race of men
Let the Plan of Love and Light work out.
And may it seal the door where evil dwells.

Let Light and Love and Power
restore the Plan on Earth.

*As taught by Tibetan master Djwhal Khul
through Alice Baily.*